First-Time Mom's
BABY
JOURNAL

"I didn't give you the gift of life,
life gave me the gift of you."

Unknown

First-Time Mom's
BABY
JOURNAL

Create a Keepsake, Record Bonding Experiences, and Stay Organized

AUBREY GROSSEN

Illustrations by
ELIZABETH GRAEBER

ROCKRIDGE
PRESS

For general information on our other products and services or to obtain technical support, please contact our Customer Care Department within the United States at (866) 744-2665, or outside the United States at (510) 253-0500.

Rockridge Press publishes its books in a variety of electronic and print formats. Some content that appears in print may not be available in electronic books, and vice versa.

TRADEMARKS: Rockridge Press and the Rockridge Press logo are trademarks or registered trademarks of Callisto Media Inc. and/or its affiliates, in the United States and other countries, and may not be used without written permission. All other trademarks are the property of their respective owners. Rockridge Press is not associated with any product or vendor mentioned in this book.

Interior & Cover Designer: Patricia Fabricant
Art Producer: Maura Boland
Editor: Emily Angell
Production Editor: Matthew Burnett

Illustration © 2019 Elizabeth Graeber
Author photo courtesy of ©brookewhittakerphotography

ISBN: Print 978-1-64611-460-3

R0

This Journal Belongs to

....

and

My Baby

....

Born on

....

Contents

YOUR
FIRST
HOURS

"Just when you think you know love,
something little comes along
and shows you
just how big it really is."

Unknown

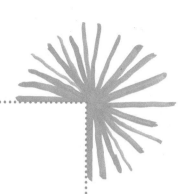

ADD
A FAVORITE PHOTO
OF YOUR BABY HERE

> *"I loved you before I knew you."*
>
> Unknown

This is how I describe the
moments leading up to your birth . . .

....

....

....

....

....

....

....

....

....

....

....

....

"Motherhood: If you think
my hands are full,
you should see my heart."

Unknown

When You Were Born

You were born weighing a perfectly

cuddly .... pounds .... ounces.

At just .... inches

or .... centimeters long,

you are the biggest thing to happen in my world.

Your place of birth is ....

....

You joined our home at your first address of

....

....

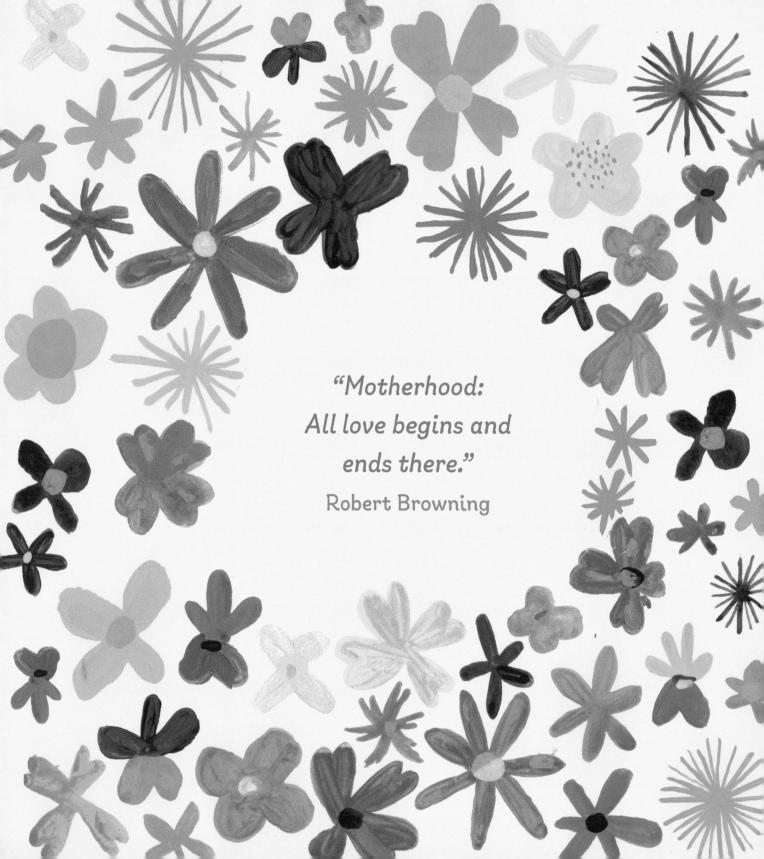

"*Motherhood:*
All love begins and
ends there."
Robert Browning

Your Birth Story

My team for your delivery included ....

....

You were born via ....

It took .... hours.

I was most excited about ....

....

I was most nervous about ....

....

The challenges I faced in birth were: ....

....

....

....

"There is nothing as powerful
as mother's love
and nothing as healing
as a child's soul."

Unknown

This is what I remember about
my birthing experience . . .

....

....

....

....

....

....

....

....

....

....

....

....

....

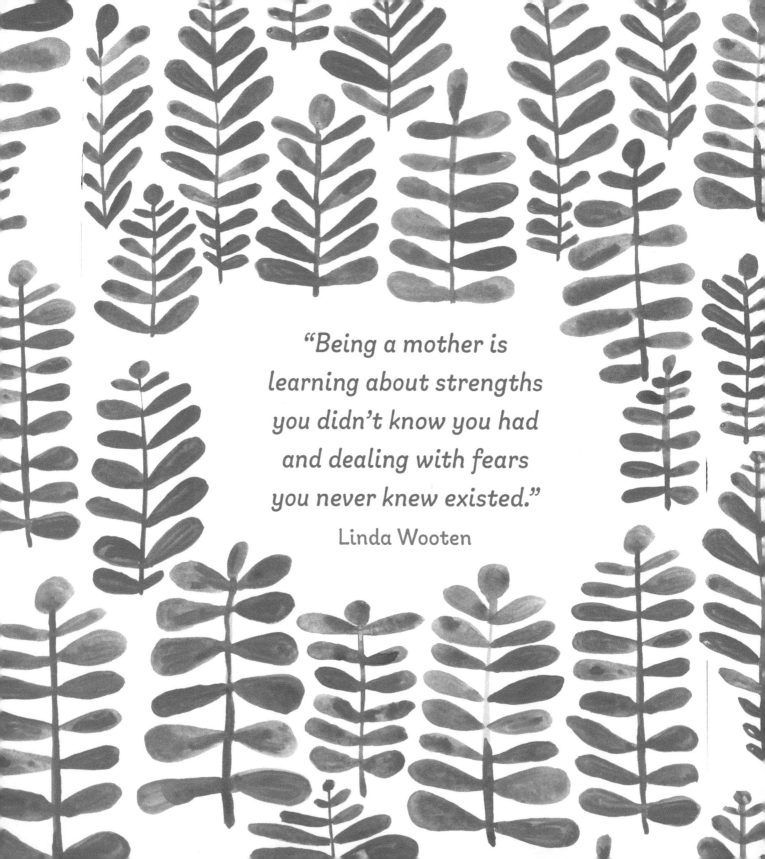

"*Being a mother is learning about strengths you didn't know you had and dealing with fears you never knew existed.*"

Linda Wooten

The moment you were born, I felt . . .

....

....

....

....

....

....

....

....

....

....

....

....

....

"Sometimes the smallest things
take up the most room in your heart."

Winnie the Pooh

Once You Were Born

When I first heard you cry, I felt ....

....

Looking at you for the first time made me feel ....

....

For your arrival, I was joined by ....

....

Their first reactions to you were ....

....

....

....

"A mother's happiness
is like a beacon, lighting up
the future but reflected
also on the past in the guise
of fond memories."

Honore de Balzac

Holding You

When I first held you, I felt ....

....

When the care team first took you from me to clean and examine

you, I thought ....

....

When they returned you to my arms, I felt ....

....

Others nearby who wanted to experience holding you were ....

....

....

When it was time for me to share your cuddles with others, I felt

....

....

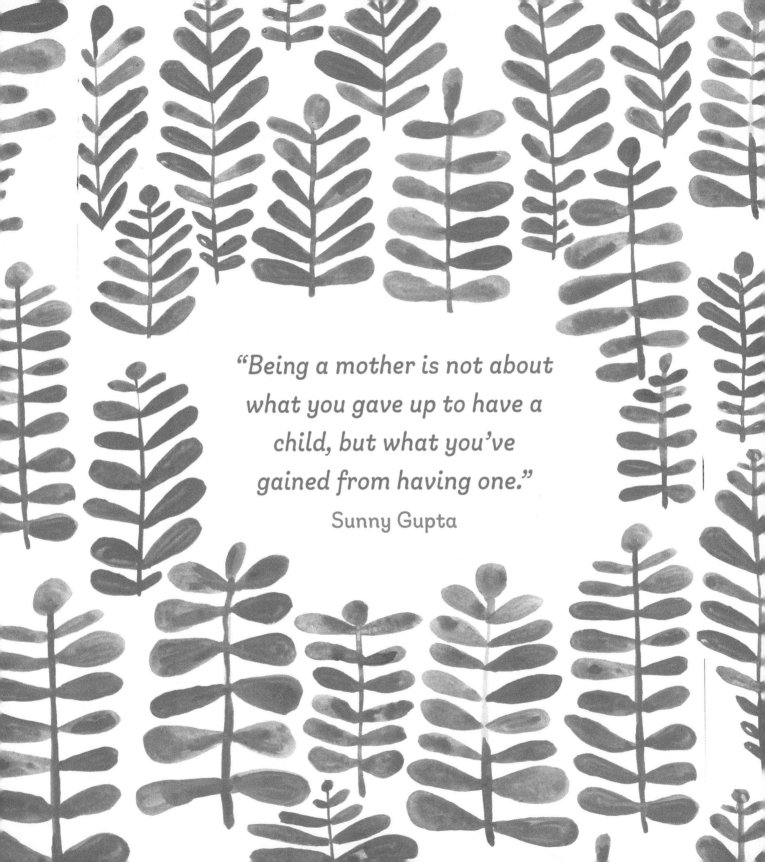

"*Being a mother is not about what you gave up to have a child, but what you've gained from having one.*"
Sunny Gupta

The first time I held you skin to skin, I felt . . .

"*Life doesn't come with a manual.
It comes with a mother.*"

Unknown

This is how you looked when I first saw you . . .

....

....

....

....

....

....

....

....

....

....

....

....

....

"A real mom:
Emotional, yet the rock.
Tired, but keeps going.
Worried, but full of hope.
Impatient, yet patient.
Overwhelmed, but never quits.
Amazing, even though doubted.
Wonderful, even in the chaos.
Life changer, every single day."

Rachel Marie Martin

The Hours After You Were Born

In your first hours experiencing life outside the womb,

your temperament seemed ....

....

You were soothed or most content when I ....

....

When .... were with you, you liked it

when they ....

You didn't like ....

....

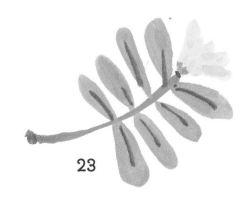

"When you love what you have,
you have everything you need."

Unknown

The presence and care of those who were with me
for your arrival meant this to me . . .

....

....

....

....

....

....

....

....

....

....

....

....

"No matter how much
I say I love you,
I always love you
more than that."

Unknown

Your First Feeding

Where and how I first fed you: ....

....

What I first fed you: ....

....

What scared me most about feeding you: ....

....

What I loved most about feeding you: ....

....

Burping a baby can be challenging. My memories of learning to
burp you are ....

....

How you responded to our first feedings together: ....

....

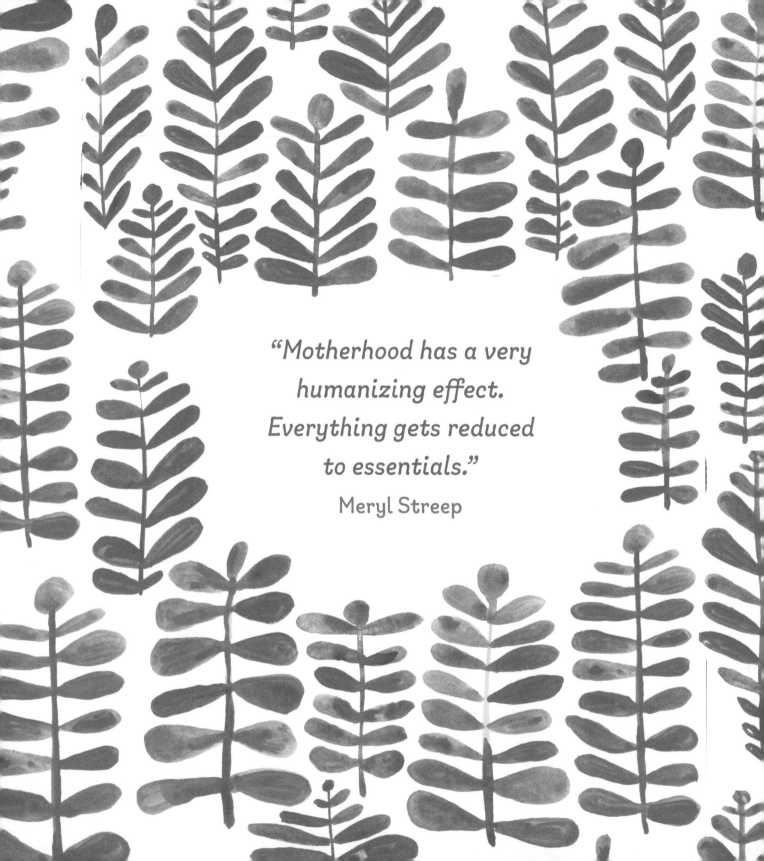

"Motherhood has a very
humanizing effect.
Everything gets reduced
to essentials."

Meryl Streep

My biggest challenges or fears as we found
our feeding rhythm were . . .

....

....

....

....

....

....

....

....

....

....

....

....

....

YOUR
FIRST
DAYS

"Having children just puts the whole world into perspective. Everything else just disappears."

Kate Winslet

Your First Baths

When and where I first bathed you: ....

....

What you liked about your bath: ....

....

What you didn't like about your bath: ....

....

The toys, soaps, lotions, and accessories I had handy for your

bath: ....

....

"When you are a mother,
you are never really alone
in your thoughts.
A mother always has
to think twice,
once for herself and
once for her child."

Sophia Loren

Who gave me advice before I bathed you: ....

....

What went best about bathing you: ....

....

What went wrong when I first bathed you: ....

....

What made me laugh during your first bath: ....

....

How you responded to your first bath: ....

....

"Love begins by taking care
of the closest ones,
the ones at home."

Mother Teresa

My memories of bathing you are . . .

....

....

....

....

....

....

....

....

....

....

....

....

....

"My mother had a great
deal of trouble with me,
but I think she enjoyed it."

Mark Twain

Your First Clothes

You arrived in this season of the year: ....

....

The first outfit you wore included these items: ....

....

You typically wore the following items at home: ....

....

....

The outfit you wore for your first special outing was ....

....

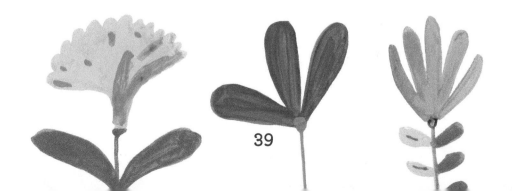

39

"A mother's love is the fuel
that enables a normal human
being to do the impossible."
Marion C. Garretty

Your very first outfit was chosen because of ....

....

Of all the tiny snaps, buttons, and zippers on your tiny clothes,

I initially struggled most with ....

....

What I found easiest about dressing you was ....

....

From concern over too-tight swaddle blankets to maneuvering

a tiny, fragile body, dressing a baby can be intimidating. What

I found scariest about dressing you was ....

....

How you looked to me when you were dressed for the first time:

....

....

"Home is where
your mom is."

Unknown

Your First Home

In your first days, your reaction to your home environment was

....

....

The place in our home you most enjoy being is ....

....

....

Some babies like their cribs, and some don't. Some don't mind the changing table, while for others it brings tears. A place in our home where you least enjoy being is ....

....

Some things that make you content and comfy at home are

....

....

*"Motherhood means
finally understanding
why Mama Bear's
porridge went cold."*

Unknown

Having a new little person at home has felt like ....

....

My favorite thing to do at home with you in the first days is

....

....

Life at home has changed in these ways: ....

....

The hardest of those changes is ....

....

The best of those changes is ....

....

*"If at the end of the day,
everyone feels loved,
you have done enough."*

Unknown

Having you home with me, in the moments when
you're sleeping quietly in my arms or in your crib,
I think about the mother I want to be to you.
This is how I describe her . . .

....

....

....

....

....

....

....

....

....

....

....

"Nothing is lost until your mother can't find it."

Unknown

From burp cloths to onesies to sleepers, we are dirtying this item of laundry most often: ....

....

Booties, caps, blankies, and more! Depending on what keeps you comfy and what we go through, I plan to have plenty of these items clean and ready to go: ....

....

It's believed that some smells are soothing to baby. The item you're using that I won't wash right away is ....

....

49

"Becoming a mother makes you realize you can do almost anything one-handed."

Unknown

The smell of your freshly washed clothes and all those tiny socks! The first time I did your laundry was like ....

....

Seeing your precious clothes come out of the dryer, reminding me how my world has changed, was like ....

....

The clothes pile up fast, and there's so much else to do! At first it's all about survival, but my thoughts on creating a system for keeping things clean and put away are ....

....

What I love most about your clothes is ....

....

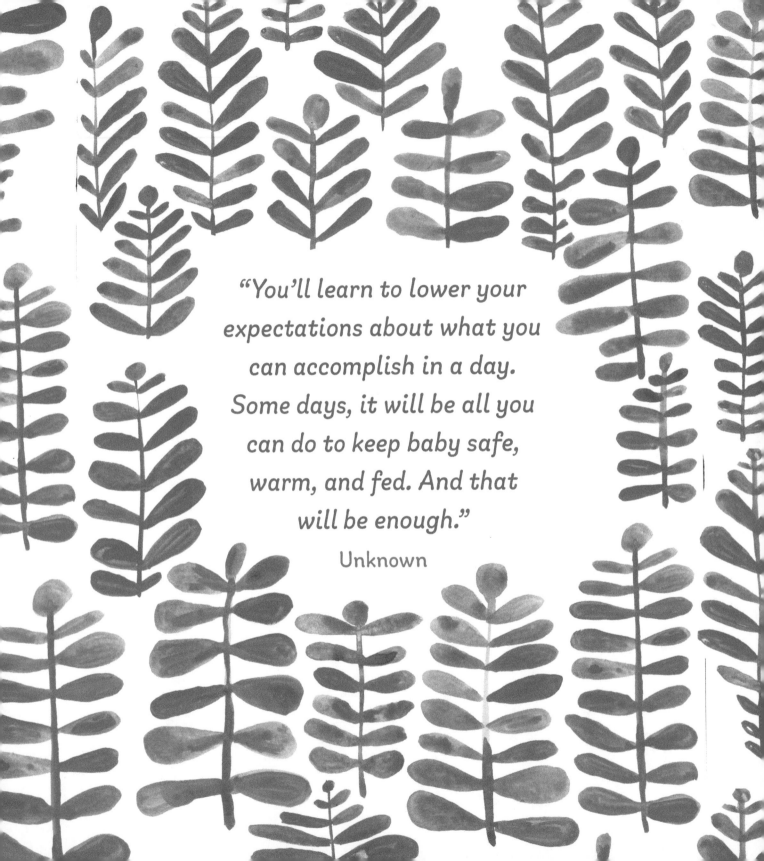

"You'll learn to lower your expectations about what you can accomplish in a day. Some days, it will be all you can do to keep baby safe, warm, and fed. And that will be enough."

Unknown

In our first days together, I've focused on you and some day-to-day things that might've once seemed mundane but keep our home going. My thoughts about how life has looked in our first days at home together are . . .

....

....

....

....

....

....

....

....

....

....

....

"Mother is a verb.
It's something you do.
Not just who you are."

Cheryl Lacey Donovan

How Your Feeding Is Progressing

In a typical feeding during your first days, you're usually taking in about .... ounces.

You're doing this about .... times per day.

With more and more practice together, hopefully our feedings are going better and better. So far, your favorite feeding position is ....

....

Whether first thing in the morning or late at night, your favorite feed of the day is ....

....

This is how you're doing with burping: ....

....

After a feeding, your favorite thing to do is ....

....

"There's no way to be
a perfect mother
and a million ways to
be a good one."

Jill Churchill

My favorite position to feed you in is ....

....

The most important thing I've learned about feeding you through

practice is ....

....

The best advice I've received from others about feeding you is

....

....

These things make me most comfortable for feeding you:

....

....

My favorite thing to do after your feedings is ....

....

....

"Taking care of yourself is part of taking care of your kids."

Unknown

When it's just you and me during nighttime feeds,
in the quiet, I think about . . .

....

....

....

....

....

....

....

....

....

....

....

....

....

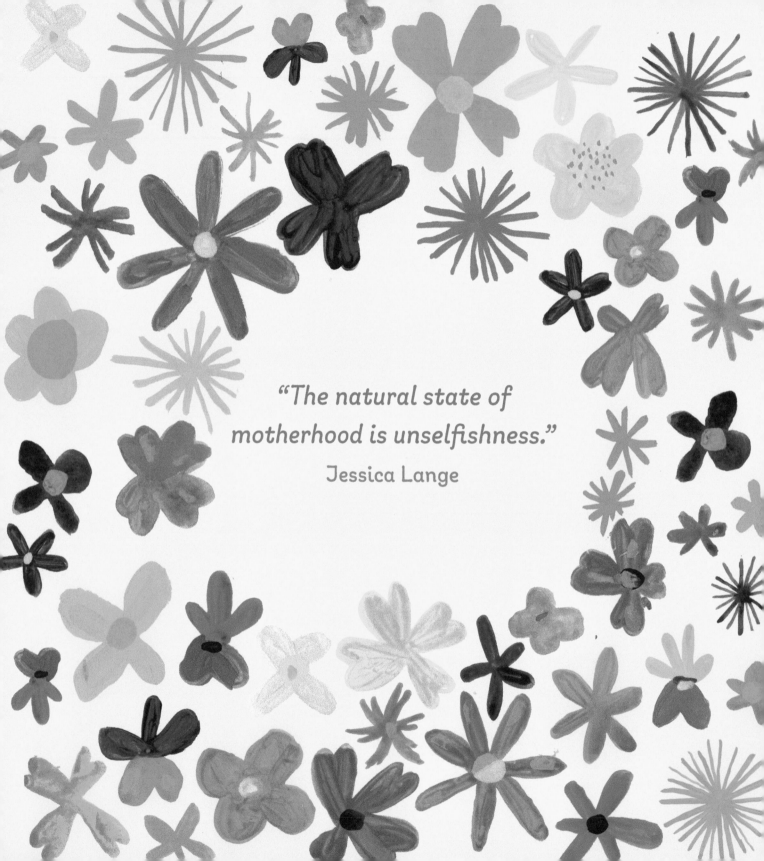

"*The natural state of motherhood is unselfishness.*"

Jessica Lange

Your Diapers

You produce about .... dirty diapers in each of your first days.

You produce about .... wet diapers in each of your first days.

Your reaction to having a dirty diaper is ....

....

Your reaction to having a wet diaper is ....

....

The part of diaper changes you handle best is ....

....

....

The part of diaper changes you dislike most is ....

....

....

"Changing a diaper is a lot
like getting a present from
your grandmother.
You're not sure what you've got,
but you're pretty sure you're
not going to like it."

Jeff Foxworthy

I've entered a place in my life where the subject of poop is common discussion. The people I most talk about this with are ....

....

Keeping track of frequency and other aspects of dirty or wet diapers is one indicator of your health. So far, this is how I'm feeling about how many and what kinds of diapers you're having:

....

....

The challenges I'm having with diapering you are ....

....

The things that are going best about diaper time are ....

....

The things I use that make diapering easier are ....

....

"The phrase 'working mother'
is redundant."

Jane Sellman

The first time I got pooped on . . .

....

....

....

....

....

....

....

....

....

....

....

....

....

"Moms are the people
who know us the best
and love us the most."

Unknown

Our First Outings

Our first outing together was to ....
....

You were dressed for the outing in this way: ....
....

Your response to riding in the car seat was ....
....

Your response to being out and about was ....
....

How you seemed when we arrived back home after your first

outing: ....
....

"It's not easy being a mother.
If it were, fathers would do it."
Dorothy, "The Golden Girls"

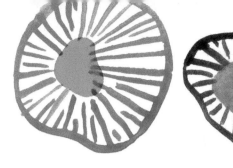

My biggest apprehension about taking you out the first time was

....

....

My biggest misconception about taking you out the first time was

....

....

What I enjoyed most about our first outing was ....

....

The hardest thing about our outing was ....

....

People's reaction to us on our first outing was ....

....

How I felt when we got home from our first outing was ....

....

"*Motherhood is
the greatest thing and
the hardest thing.*"

Ricki Lake

The truth about our first outings together,
just you and me, is . . .

....

....

....

....

....

....

....

....

....

....

....

....

"If I know what love is,
it is because of you."

Hermann Hesse

Your First Doctor Visit

This is how I'd describe your first visit with your
pediatrician and how I felt about it . . .

....

....

....

....

....

....

....

....

....

"A mother's arms are
made of tenderness
and children sleep
soundly in them."

Victor Hugo

Your First Sleep

You sleep about .... hours in each of your first days.

Your nighttime sleep is like ....
....

Your daytime sleep is like ....
....

I put you to sleep on your ....
....

Practicing safe sleep, you sleep in your ...., and it is devoid
of any items that could cause you harm, like ....
....

You seem to enjoy .... right before you go to sleep.

75

"Being a mom has made me
so tired. And so happy."

Tina Fey

In your first days at home, your sleeping schedule impacted mine in this way: ....

....

This is how I feel about my new sleeping schedule: ....

....

The things I'm doing to adapt are ....

....

The things I'm doing to survive lack of sleep are ....

....

The things I'm doing to replenish my body are ....

....

My favorite thing to do when you nap is ....

....

77

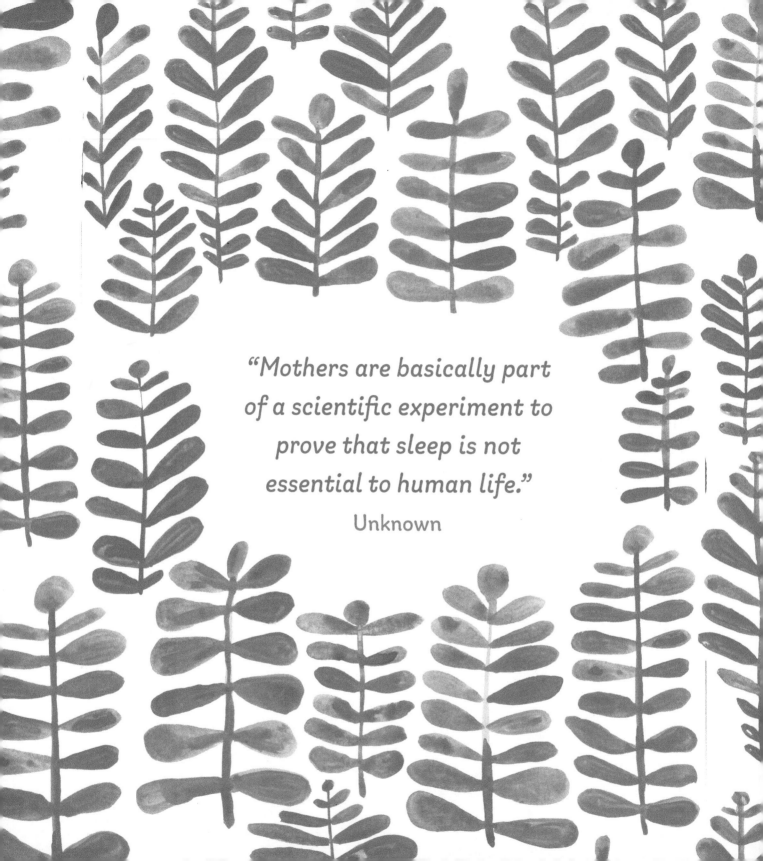

"Mothers are basically part of a scientific experiment to prove that sleep is not essential to human life."

Unknown

I never knew how much I loved sleep.
My life of little sleep feels like . . .

YOUR
FIRST
WEEKS

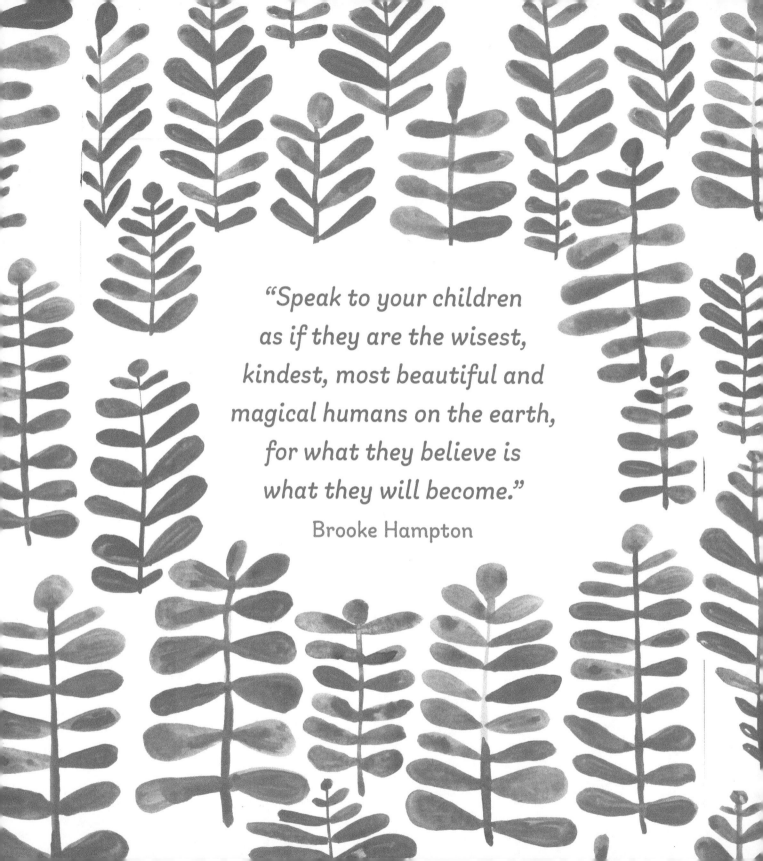

"Speak to your children
as if they are the wisest,
kindest, most beautiful and
magical humans on the earth,
for what they believe is
what they will become."

Brooke Hampton

Babies change so fast. In your first weeks,
I've noticed the following changes in you . . .

....

....

....

....

....

....

....

....

....

....

....

....

"A mom's hug lasts
long after she lets go."

Unknown

Your Favorite Things

In the early weeks since you were brought home, the things that

make you happiest are ....

....

Besides me, the person who has the special touch to soothe you is

....

....

Your first favorite toy is ....

....

Your first favorite book is ....

....

Your first favorite position to be held in is ....

....

"I'm proud of many things in life,
but nothing beats being a mother."

Unknown

My Favorite Things

My favorite place in our home to be with you is ....

..............................., where we ....

....•

When I'm able to take five minutes to myself, I usually go ....

..............................., where I ....

....•

If I could change something about our house or home environment

since bringing you home to make it work better for our new life,

it would be ....

....•

What I'm most grateful for about our home is ....

....•

"Behind every great kid
is a mom who's pretty sure
she's screwing it all up."

Unknown

Your First Cries

Your first cry that made me cry was ....

....

What eventually made you feel better was ....

....

The first thing you did that made me panic was ....

....

The first thing you did that made me laugh so hard was ....

....

"We have a secret in our culture,
and it's not that birth is painful.
It's that women are strong."

Laura Stavoe Harm

The first thing I did that made you cry was ....

....

The most embarrassing question I asked the doctor was ....

....

In the first weeks, I must have called the doctor's office

.... times.

My favorite nurse at your doctor's office is ....

because ....

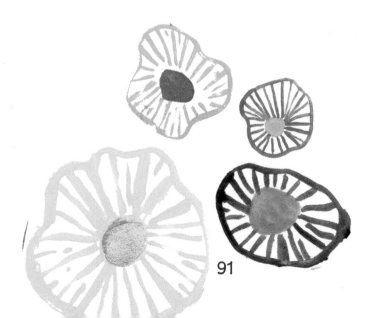

91

"Motherhood is filled
with magical little
moments that bring
you immense joy."

Namrata Shirodkar

The first time I struggled to soothe you in the ways that usually worked was when ....

....

Since then, I learned to try ....

....,

which now helps you feel better. I know that you'll continue to change, and so my methods will have to keep changing, too. Besides me, of course, you most enjoy cuddles from ....

....

Their bond with you is like ....

....

The first time you genuinely smiled was ....

in response to ....

....

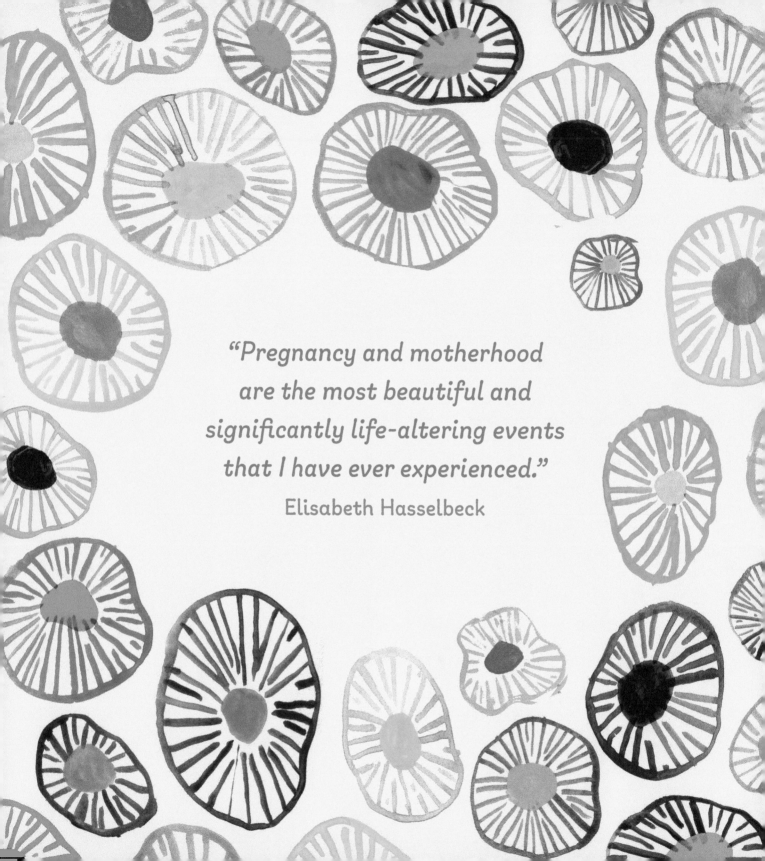

"Pregnancy and motherhood
are the most beautiful and
significantly life-altering events
that I have ever experienced."

Elisabeth Hasselbeck

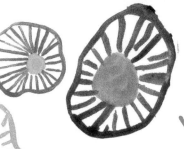

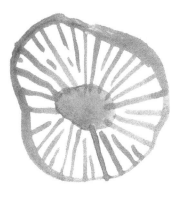

Your First Smile

When you first smiled, I felt ....

....

I laughed so hard when you first ....

....

The new baby gear I've most struggled to operate is ....

....

The first time I felt truly embarrassed by something I did as a mom

was when ....

....

The first nickname I gave you is ....

....

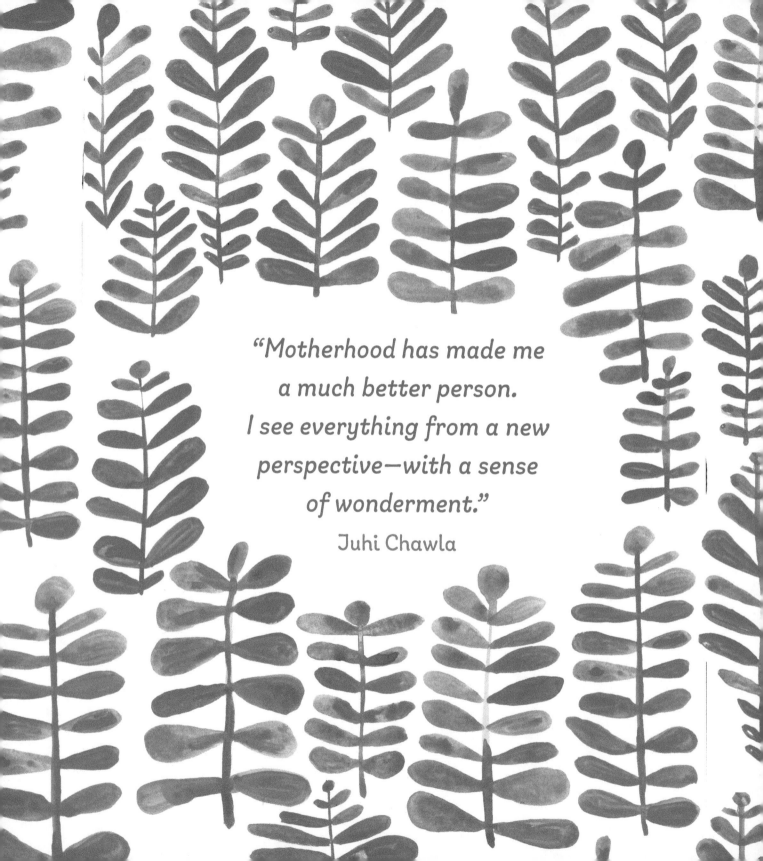

"Motherhood has made me a much better person. I see everything from a new perspective—with a sense of wonderment."

Juhi Chawla

So far, my favorite thing about being your mom is . . .

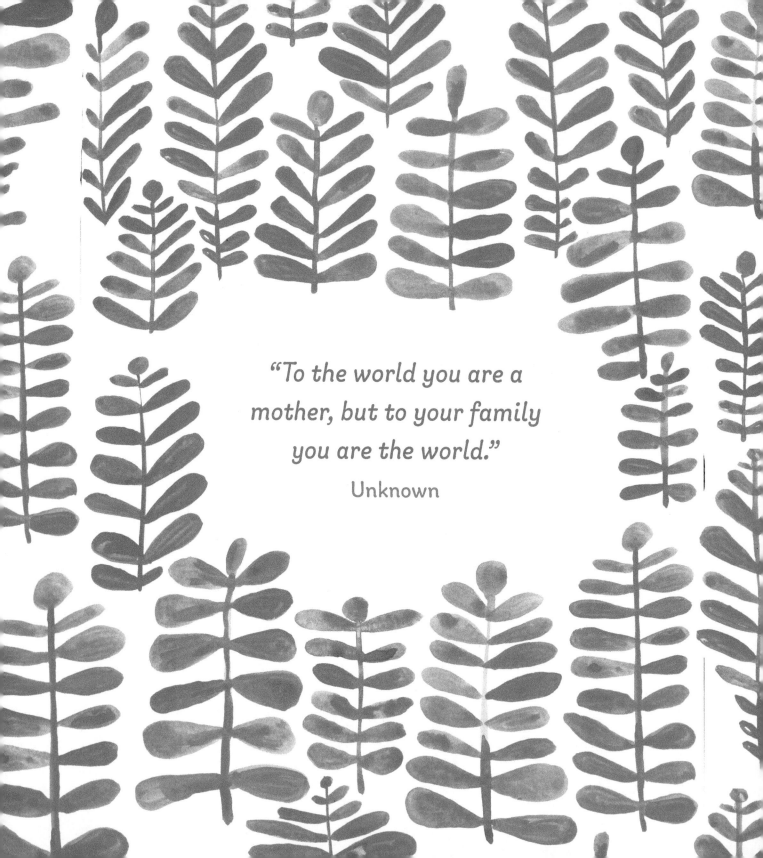

"To the world you are a
mother, but to your family
you are the world."

Unknown

Whether longing for it to speed up or slow down,
this is how I now feel about time . . .

....

....

....

....

....

....

....

....

....

....

....

....

YOUR
FIRST
MONTHS

"*Motherhood is such an
evolving journey.*"

Solange Knowles

You Are Growing and Changing

Whether you were born bald or with a head full of curls, whether you, at birth, resembled Mom or Dad, you've changed.

In your first weeks after birth, you looked ....
....

As months have passed, you've changed physically in this way:
....
....

When we are out in public, people sometimes comment about your ....
....

Your cutest expressions are made under these circumstances:
....
....

"Having kids—the responsibility of rearing good, kind, ethical, responsible human beings—is the biggest job anyone can embark on."

Maria Shriver

Each part of you is precious to me, but some of your cutest physical characteristics are ....

My favorite characteristic you share with a loved one is ....

When you were born, your eyes were ...., and now they're the color ....

The first time I looked at you and felt that time was moving too fast was when ....

"*Yoga pants. Because
parenting is
a full-contact sport.*"

Unknown

Something I used to do before
I was a mom that I now miss is . . .

....

....

....

....

....

....

....

....

....

....

....

....

"If evolution really works,
how come mothers only
have two hands?"

Milton Berle

From the time you were born to now, this part of your developing traits and personality has most surprised me: ....

....

A place we go together where you love to explore is ....

....

The personality traits you have now that I predict will be valuable in your future are ....

....

The observations of others that stoke my pride as your mom are

....

....

The things you're now doing that seem to give you pride are

....

....

"To describe my mother would be to write about a hurricane in its perfect power. Or the climbing, falling colors of a rainbow."

Maya Angelou

So far, the things about motherhood I've struggled with most are

....

....

The things about motherhood I take the most pride in are ....

....

My biggest goals for myself in motherhood, as things progress, are

....

....

If I've experienced any postpartum depression, anxiety, or fatigue,

my path to healing is ....

....

"Motherhood is far
better than I expected.
I love it with
all of my heart."
Ayesha Curry

The first time I felt like I was really getting the hang of this

mothering thing was when ....

....

Then you ...., and I felt like I had to

learn things all over again.

The difference between my mothering at the beginning and my

mothering now is ....

....

The things I now most enjoy about being a mother are ....

....

"A mother's love endures
through all."

Washington Irving

Something I never want to forget
about this time in life is . . .

....

....

....

....

....

....

....

....

....

....

....

....

"A mother is not a person
to lean on, but a person
to make leaning unnecessary."
Dorothy Canfield Fisher

My Biggest Hopes for Your Future Are . . .

....

....

....

....

....

....

....

....

....

....

117

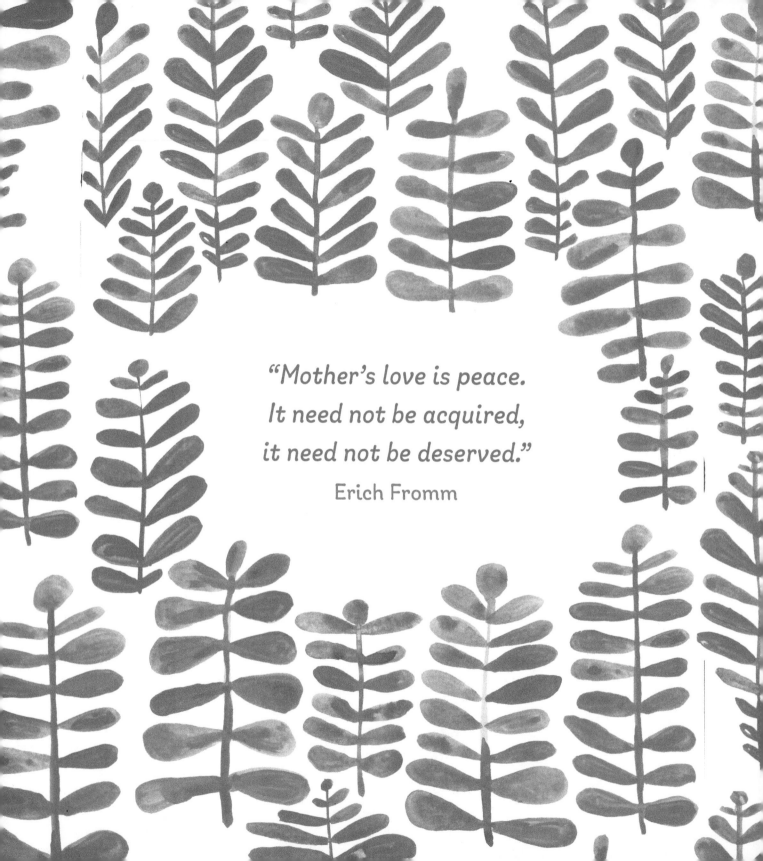

"Mother's love is peace.
It need not be acquired,
it need not be deserved."

Erich Fromm

What it means to me to be your mother . . .

MAJOR MILESTONES AND HANDY LISTS

Major Milestones

Use these pages to help you track your and baby's progress and stay organized.

Your first bath at home was in .... Date: ....

Your first smile happened when .... Date: ....

The first time you rolled over was on .... Date: ....

The first time you sat up was on .... Date: ....

Your first long stretch of sleep was in .... Date: ....

The first time you crawled was on .... Date: ....

Your first visible tooth was .... Date: ....

The first solid food you tried was .... Date: ....

The first time you clapped was .... Date: ....

The first time you waved was .... Date: ....

The first time you pointed was .... Date: ....

Your first babble was .... Date: ....

Your first laugh happened when .... Date: ....

The first time you responded to your name was .... Date: ....

The first time you fed yourself was .... Date: ....

The first vacation I took you on was .... Date: ....

So far the longest stretch you sleep is ....

....

Your favorite physical activity seems to be ....

....

Your favorite book is ....

....

The toys that make you the happiest are ....

....

Of eating, listening to music, dancing, playing with blocks, or any
activity, your favorite seems to be ....

....

Your first word was .... Date: ....

The furniture you first cruised was .... Date: ....

Your first independent step was taken in .... Date: ....

Feeding List

Use these pages to help you stay nourished and comfortable during feedings.

◊ If I'm breastfeeding, I'm making sure to eat plenty and drink extra water to keep up with the demand on my body.

◊ I have a good supply of my favorite snacks, like

◊ Nuts

◊ Chopped fruit and veggies

◊ Granola Bars

◊ Cheese

◊ Crackers

◊ Food you can eat one-handed

◊ I've consulted the hospital lactation consultant and friends who can offer support and advice. My advocates and support team are (on the lines below list friends, family, a partner, doula/midwife, other moms, and anyone else you can count on):

....

....

....

....

◇ Whether breastfeeding or formula feeding, I'm calling on others to help with feedings when possible. Help can be in the form of:

　　◇ Prepping a bottle

　　◇ Giving a bottle

　　◇ Taking care of baby so that I can rest when needed

　　◇ Cleaning

　　◇ Making food for mom

　　◇ Other help ....

◇ I have all the bottling things, cleaning things, and personal care items I need stocked and ready to go. Those things include:

....

....

....

....

....

....

◇ I also have a soft toy or blanket and a good feeding pillow to help keep baby comfortable during feedings.

Home Sweet Home List

Use these pages to help you stay organized at home.

◊ The changing area contains all the essentials:

   ◊ Diapers

   ◊ Wipes

   ◊ Creams

   ◊ Extra clothes

   ◊ Baggies for diaper disposal

   ◊ A safe place to put baby when I need to put them down

   ◊ Toy or object to distract baby while I clean up

Sometimes I wish I had extra sets of hands to do this kind of maneuvering!

◊ Our home is outfitted for my and baby's comfort, with plenty of the following:

   ◊ Toys

   ◊ Blankets

   ◊ Books

   ◊ Calming music

   ◊ Snacks for Mom

   ◊ PJs and comfy clothing

◊ Telephone numbers for my and baby's doctors and baby's after-hours emergency contacts, whether displayed on the fridge, or saved in my phone, are always accessible. These numbers include:

◊ ....

....

....

....

◊ ....

....

....

....

◊ ....

....

....

....

Outings List

Use these pages to help you stay organized on outings.

◊ Baby's bag is fully stocked so that we're prepared before we leave the house, especially if we have to pop out on a moment's notice—including disposable wipes, plastic bags for trash, a change of clothes, and toys to distract baby.

◊ In baby's bag I've placed a change of clothes for me—I won't be caught out when there's an inevitable volcanic spit-up or diaper explosion!

◊ I also make sure to have a changing pad in case I can't find a restroom with a changing table. In a pinch, the floor, a chair, or even my lap will do!

◊ If I'm nursing, I keep a baby sling or coverup handy in case that's how I'm most comfortable feeding in public. Baby can become hungry at any moment!

◊ I have familiarized myself with all the equipment we need for our outing, from car seat to stroller and more.

◊ Use the following lines to list any additional gear or supplies you will need while you are out.

◊ ....
....
....
....
◊ ....
....
....
....
◊ ....
....
....
....
◊ ....
....
....
....

Skills and Activities

Use these pages to track your and baby's progress with skills and activities.

Skills and Activities My Baby Enjoys and Has Mastered

....

....

....

....

Skills and Activities We're Working on Together That Are Most Challenging

....

....

....

....

Skills and Activities We're Working on Together That We Find the Most Fun

....

....

....

....

Skills and Activities That We'll Work on Soon

....

....

....

....

Baby's Doctor Visits

If not *the* first, one of your first outings with baby is sure to be your first trip to the pediatrician's office. Use this chart to help keep track of the visits, your concerns, and baby's milestones.

Date	Doctor Seen	Mom's Notes or Baby's Milestones (height/weight)
....	....	....
....	....	....
....	....	....
....	....	....
....	....	....
....	....	....
....	....	....
....	....	....
....	....	....
....	....	....

Date	Doctor Seen	Mom's Notes or Baby's Milestones (height/weight)
....	....	....
....	....	....
....	....	....
....	....	....
....	....	....
....	....	....
....	....	....
....	....	....
....	....	....
....	....	....
....	....	....
....	....	....
....	....	....
....	....	....

Food You've Tried

Use these pages to help you track baby's progress with trying new food.

Date	Type of Food	Baby's Reaction
....	....	....
....	....	....
....	....	....
....	....	....
....	....	....
....	....	....
....	....	....
....	....	....
....	....	....
....	....	....
....	....	....
....	....	....

Date	Type of Food	Baby's Reaction
....	....	....
....	....	....
....	....	....
....	....	....
....	....	....
....	....	....
....	....	....
....	....	....
....	....	....
....	....	....
....	....	....
....	....	....

From Feeding to Sleeping—
Our Daily Schedule

Use the following charts to track your baby's feeding, sleeping, play, and diaper changes each day for one month. In the Feed box you can include how many ounces of milk baby had, which breast you used if breastfeeding (L=Left and R=Right), and for how long.
In the Diaper box you can include a 'B' for Bowel Movement or a "W" for Wet Diaper.
In the Sleep and Play boxes you can record how long your baby slept and played.

DATE:	MORNING	AFTERNOON	EVENING	NIGHT
Feed				
Sleep				
Play				
Diaper				

DATE:	MORNING	AFTERNOON	EVENING	NIGHT
Feed				
Sleep				
Play				
Diaper				

DATE:	MORNING	AFTERNOON	EVENING	NIGHT
Feed				
Sleep				
Play				
Diaper				

DATE:	MORNING	AFTERNOON	EVENING	NIGHT
Feed				
Sleep				
Play				
Diaper				

DATE:	MORNING	AFTERNOON	EVENING	NIGHT
Feed				
Sleep				
Play				
Diaper				

DATE:	MORNING	AFTERNOON	EVENING	NIGHT
Feed				
Sleep				
Play				
Diaper				

DATE:	MORNING	AFTERNOON	EVENING	NIGHT
Feed				
Sleep				
Play				
Diaper				

DATE:	MORNING	AFTERNOON	EVENING	NIGHT
Feed				
Sleep				
Play				
Diaper				

DATE:	MORNING	AFTERNOON	EVENING	NIGHT
Feed				
Sleep				
Play				
Diaper				

DATE:	MORNING	AFTERNOON	EVENING	NIGHT
Feed				
Sleep				
Play				
Diaper				

DATE:	MORNING	AFTERNOON	EVENING	NIGHT
Feed				
Sleep				
Play				
Diaper				

DATE:	MORNING	AFTERNOON	EVENING	NIGHT
Feed				
Sleep				
Play				
Diaper				

DATE:	MORNING	AFTERNOON	EVENING	NIGHT
Feed				
Sleep				
Play				
Diaper				

DATE:	MORNING	AFTERNOON	EVENING	NIGHT
Feed				
Sleep				
Play				
Diaper				

DATE:	MORNING	AFTERNOON	EVENING	NIGHT
Feed				
Sleep				
Play				
Diaper				

DATE:	MORNING	AFTERNOON	EVENING	NIGHT
Feed				
Sleep				
Play				
Diaper				

DATE:	MORNING	AFTERNOON	EVENING	NIGHT
Feed				
Sleep				
Play				
Diaper				

DATE:	MORNING	AFTERNOON	EVENING	NIGHT
Feed				
Sleep				
Play				
Diaper				

DATE:	MORNING	AFTERNOON	EVENING	NIGHT
Feed				
Sleep				
Play				
Diaper				

DATE:	MORNING	AFTERNOON	EVENING	NIGHT
Feed				
Sleep				
Play				
Diaper				

DATE:	MORNING	AFTERNOON	EVENING	NIGHT
Feed				
Sleep				
Play				
Diaper				

DATE:	MORNING	AFTERNOON	EVENING	NIGHT
Feed				
Sleep				
Play				
Diaper				

DATE:	MORNING	AFTERNOON	EVENING	NIGHT
Feed				
Sleep				
Play				
Diaper				

DATE:	MORNING	AFTERNOON	EVENING	NIGHT
Feed				
Sleep				
Play				
Diaper				

DATE:	MORNING	AFTERNOON	EVENING	NIGHT
Feed				
Sleep				
Play				
Diaper				

DATE:	MORNING	AFTERNOON	EVENING	NIGHT
Feed				
Sleep				
Play				
Diaper				

DATE:	MORNING	AFTERNOON	EVENING	NIGHT
Feed				
Sleep				
Play				
Diaper				

DATE:	MORNING	AFTERNOON	EVENING	NIGHT
Feed				
Sleep				
Play				
Diaper				

DATE:	MORNING	AFTERNOON	EVENING	NIGHT
Feed				
Sleep				
Play				
Diaper				

DATE:	MORNING	AFTERNOON	EVENING	NIGHT
Feed				
Sleep				
Play				
Diaper				

DATE:	MORNING	AFTERNOON	EVENING	NIGHT
Feed				
Sleep				
Play				
Diaper				

YOUR FIRST PHOTOS

ADD A FAVORITE PHOTO
OF YOUR BABY HERE

....

....

ADD A FAVORITE PHOTO
OF YOUR BABY HERE

....

....

ADD A FAVORITE PHOTO
OF YOUR BABY HERE

ADD A FAVORITE PHOTO
OF YOUR BABY HERE

ADD A FAVORITE PHOTO
OF YOUR BABY HERE

ADD A FAVORITE PHOTO
OF YOUR BABY HERE

ADD A FAVORITE PHOTO
OF YOUR BABY HERE

ADD A FAVORITE PHOTO
OF YOUR BABY HERE

About the Author

AUBREY GROSSEN is a wife and a mama to three kids. After having her first baby, she suffered through postpartum depression. As a result, she created an online community. It started off with thirty-nine close friends and family members, and over the years, it has grown to tens of thousands of moms. Writing and creating are her outlets, and she has grown her blogging business since 2014. She blogs regularly on *The Mamahood Blog* (themamahoodblog.com), is a co-host for *The Mamahood Podcast*, and loves hosting events and retreats for moms everywhere.

Motherhood hasn't always been something that comes naturally for her, but it has been one of the greatest blessings in her life. She fought through a rough patch of pregnancies and miscarriages to get her babies here. She finds joy in traveling with her family, spending time with her kids and husband, and having a bowl of late-night ice cream in bed while watching her favorite shows with her husband.

CPSIA information can be obtained
at www.ICGtesting.com
Printed in the USA
BVHW051453050220
571530BV00011B/436